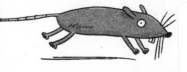

# WOULD YOU RATHER? TUDORS

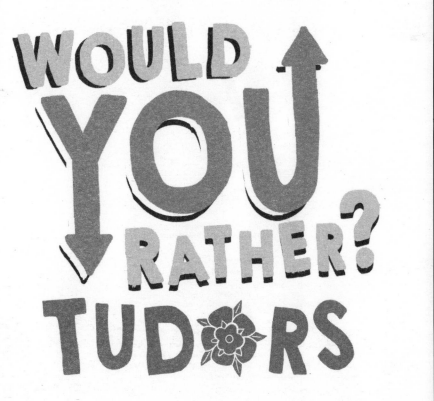

First published in Great Britain 2024 by Red Shed, part of Farshore

An imprint of HarperCollins*Publishers*
1 London Bridge Street, London SE1 9GF
www.farshore.co.uk

HarperCollins*Publishers*
Macken House, 39/40 Mayor Street Upper,
Dublin 1, D01 C9W8

Written by Clive Gifford
Illustrated by Tim Wesson
Copyright © HarperCollins*Publishers* Limited 2024
ISBN 978 0 00 859930 0
Printed and bound in the UK using 100% Renewable Electricity at CPI Group (UK) Ltd.
001

A CIP catalogue record for this title is available from the British Library.

This book contains FSC™ certified paper and other controlled
sources to ensure responsible forest management.

For more information visit: www.harpercollins.co.uk/green

CLIVE GIFFORD • TIM WESSON

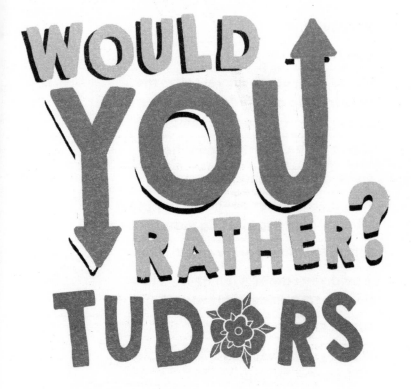

WOULD YOU RATHER? TUDORS

RED SHED

# Contents

# Introduction

When you think of Tudor England, what pops into your mind? King Henry VIII and his wives? Massive lacy ruffs? People in stocks having mouldy, stinky vegetables thrown at them? Jousting competitions?

You'd be right – but there was much, much more! The Tudor royal family ruled England from 1485–1603. During their time in charge, there were bold battles, incredible new inventions and some seriously unusual fashions and foods.

This book is jam-packed with mind-boggling 'would you rather' questions and fascinating facts to whisk you back in time to Tudor palaces, cities, battlefields, toilets and beyond, to find out what life was really like there . . .

## Are you ready?

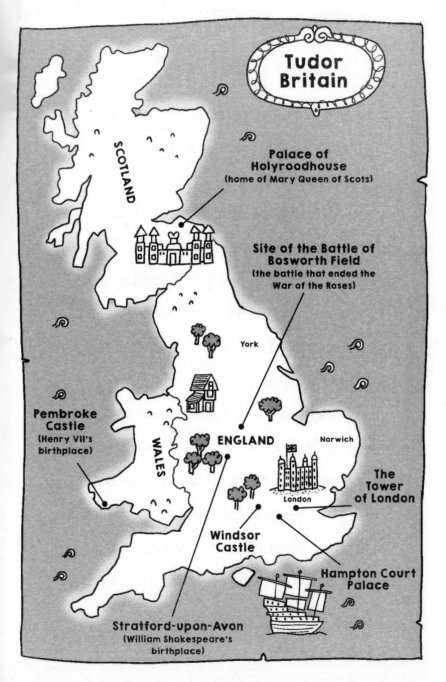

Tudor Britain

SCOTLAND

Palace of
Holyroodhouse
(home of Mary Queen of Scots)

Site of the Battle of
Bosworth Field
(the battle that ended the
War of the Roses)

York

Pembroke
Castle
(Henry VII's
birthplace)

WALES

ENGLAND

Norwich

The
Tower
of London

London

Windsor
Castle

Hampton Court
Palace

Stratford-upon-Avon
(William Shakespeare's
birthplace)

# How it all started

Before the Tudors, there was lots of competition over who should rule England, and two different parts of the royal family ended up fighting it out for the top job. On one side was the House of York, on the other was the House of Lancaster. There was NO WAY either side was going to let the other get their bottoms on the throne.

After 30 years of biffing and thumping from 1455–1485, the two sides met for one final big bash at Bosworth Field, in central England. Heading up the Yorkist army was the king, Richard III. His opponents were led by Henry Tudor from the House of Lancaster.

Richard's army was bigger than Henry's, but as the battle raged, Richard realised that his side was doing very, very badly. He desperately tried to kill Henry, but got killed himself before he'd got closer than a couple of swords lengths. With their king dead, the Yorkist army crumbled.

With that, Henry Tudor became ... King Henry VII! The victorious Lancastrian married Elizabeth of York (a Yorkist, surprise, surprise), which put a stop to all the fighting. The House of Tudor was now firmly on the throne. It was time for the Tudor age to start ...

# WOULD YOU RATHER

## shovel soil in the countryside as a Tudor farmer

OR shovel poo in the city as a toilet emptier?

DO YOU LIKE BEING OUT IN THE COUNTRYSIDE? BACK
IN TUDOR TIMES, NO ONE WORKED AS AN INFLUENCER,
RADIO DJ, OR IN A CALL CENTRE. NINE OUT OF TEN
TUDORS WORKED ON THE LAND, GROWING CROPS TO EAT
AND TENDING THEIR LIVESTOCK. IT WAS HARD WORK, NO
DOUBT ABOUT IT. BUT THAT DIDN'T MEAN THOSE WORKING
IN TUDOR CITIES GOT OFF LIGHTLY . . .

# Shovel soil as a Tudor farmer

Did you choose a life of pigpens and sheep shearing? *Baaaa*-d luck. Farming as a Tudor peasant was HARD.

Some slightly richer farmers owned their land, but many peasants would have to rent from a local lord or landowner, paying with money and a share of what crops they grew.

All farm work would be done by hand, perhaps with the odd horse or oxen to help. There were no tractors or combine harvesters to make life easier. You'd need good weather, too. Bad weather meant bad harvests – which meant no food. Summer and autumn would be busy growing and harvesting food to get through winter – remember, there were no fridges or freezers, so you'd need to get pickling to preserve your dinners. Poaching (stealing) rabbits, birds or fish from your lord's land was an option – but expect punishment if you were caught!

Life as a peasant was unlikely to improve, and it could get much worse, especially if your lord raised your rent or took back the land for himself.

# Shovel poo as a toilet emptier

Did you choose to get up close and personal with some Tudor toilets? *Urine* for a treat, if you can stomach a seriously STINKY job . . .

Visitors to Tudor castles would naturally need to relieve themselves. These buildings would channel all of the poo down chutes into a large, smelly hole called a cesspit. Toilet emptiers would have to clean them out, using just a bucket and their hands (perhaps a shovel if they were lucky), then cart the stinky load away. *Poo* had better believe it: it would be a big job. Some castles only emptied their cesspit once every two or three years. Tudor toilet emptiers also got an unusual job title into the bargain – gong farmers!

Did they go about banging and rattling gongs while other people did their business? Nope, wrong type of gong. The name came from the old English word *gang*, meaning 'to go'. The poo that gong farmers collected was called 'nightsoil' – a polite Tudor word for poo!

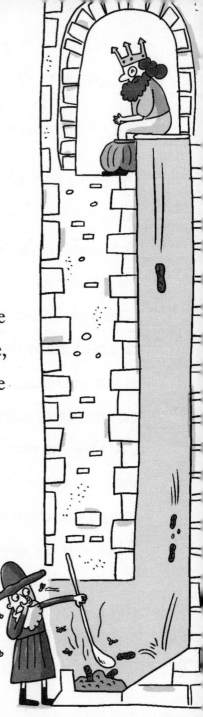

Where did this name come from, you ask? This one's got an easy answer – gong farmers only worked at night. Probably just as well . . . you could avoid the embarrassment of being seen neck-deep in poo in the daylight. *Yuck*!

If you had a gong farmer for a parent, watch out – you might end up joining them at work. Small children were useful at getting into the tiny, stinky corners of cesspits that adults couldn't reach.

Gong farmers would then haul all the mess away by horse and cart and take it out of the city and into the countryside. They'd sell their cartloads of waste to farmers who would spread it on their fields to help crops grow.

These hard-working shovellers played a vital part in keeping England clean, but they earned just pennies for each tonne of poo they collected. No fair!

This STINKS!

**Being a gong farmer wasn't the only poo-related job in Tudor England. Turn to page 52 to find out more . . .**

# TUDOR EXTRAS
## Rotten remedies

Welcome to the Tudor doctor! Prepare yourself for some toe-curling cures that you definitely wouldn't get in a pharmacy today . . . don't try these at home!

### Cure for baldness

Mix wine, cow's milk and children's wee together and then wash your head with the mixture. As an alternative, try shampooing your scalp with crushed beetles!

## Cure for bed-wetting

Drink a soup made from cooked boar's hooves, then eat the tongues of three geese. Wash this all down with a drink of mashed up snails mixed into wine. What a monstrous meal!

## Cure for a cough or asthma

Cover some live spiders in butter and then swallow them whole. At least the butter would taste nice . . .

## Cure for nosebleeds or cuts

Lay a spider's web over the cut or bleeding nose. This wasn't actually a terrible idea – some spider's webs have antibacterial properties.

## Whooping cough

This common Tudor lung infection mostly affected babies and children. There were a large number of very strange cures for whooping cough . . . it's likely that few of them actually worked. Here are a few you might have ended up trying:

**1.**
Go into a barn and breathe in the bad breath of a cow, sheep or horse.

**2.**
Be passed under and over a braying donkey.

**3.**

Wear a live caterpillar in a tiny bag around your neck for weeks until the caterpillar dies.

**4.**

Drink a syrup made from snails mixed with sugar, or gulp down soup made from boiled owls.

**5.**

Go out into a field at sunset and have your head placed in a hole in the ground. We don't know how long you'd be stuck there!

# Mega monarchs hall of fame

Welcome to the Tudor hall of fame, for the mega monarchs who ruled from the start of the time period right to the end. There were three kings and three queens in total (not including their various husbands and wives) – and they all had their own quirks, hobbies, friends and enemies.

Once you've finished, it's time for you to decide – which king or queen's reign would you have preferred to live under?

# Henry VII
## 1457-1509

Henry Tudor was the original king of the dynasty. He even gave it his name!

In the 1400s, the Wars of the Roses had been raging in England. Two powerful groups, the House of York and the House of Lancaster, both thought they deserved the top spot, as they had royal family ties. (Each of their families used a rose as its symbol, giving the war its name.) They fought it out until 1485, when Henry Tudor (of Lancaster) defeated Richard III (of York). After this successful battling, Henry quickly married Elizabeth of the House of York to unite the country (though no one asked her opinion about it). But even with his new wife, Henry still had to deal with rebellions from people who still supported the House of York.

He was known as a strict and stingy ruler who forced people to pay ALL their taxes. He avoided expensive wars abroad and, as a result, by the time he died, England was rich, rich, RICH!

# Henry VIII
## 1491-1547

You might have heard of this Henry already! One of the most famous Tudors, he was a larger-than-life character. In fact, he was so large that in his later years he couldn't stand up without help. He caused quite a commotion during his rule – the Catholic church wouldn't let him divorce his first wife, Catherine of Aragon, so he formed a whole new church: the Protestant Church of England. Dramatic exit!

A dashing sportsman as a young man, Henry had six wives in total (head to page 56 for more about them) and three children who became rulers (Edward, Mary and Elizabeth). He also spent and gambled so heavily that he made England poor, poor, POOR!

## Bonus fact

Henry VIII had 55 royal palaces in total. How many houses does a king need?!

# Edward VI
## 1537-1553

Boy king Edward was only nine when his father, Henry VIII, died. He became ruler, but was far too young to rule. His uncle, the Duke of Somerset, took charge in his place at first, but his ideas were unpopular, so he was executed – ouch! The Duke of Northumberland then stepped in instead.

Edward was a bright kid who could read Greek, Latin and French, and he carried on his dad's Church of England religious reforms. But he suffered from many illnesses (not exactly unusual in Tudor England). In 1553, Edward fell foul of a nasty lung disease, most likely tuberculosis, and died at aged 15. This plunged England into a struggle for power. Turn the page to find out more . . .

## Bonus fact
Edward passed laws meaning church services were held in English instead of Latin so ordinary people could understand them.

# Lady Jane Grey
## 1537-1554

Poor Lady Jane, caught up in the politics of Tudor England. Edward VI nominated her as his heir, as he was keen to stop his Catholic sister Mary from reversing all the decisions he had made to develop the Protestant church. Lady Jane shared his religion, so seemed like a safe pair of hands . . . but all did not go to plan. Rebellions and plotting saw Mary I replace her after just nine days. Lady Jane never even got to be properly crowned! In July 1553, Jane was locked in the Tower of London. She was beheaded early the following year.

## Bonus fact

Lady Jane's servants were too upset to blindfold her for her execution, so she did it herself – but then struggled to find the chopping block to put her head on.

# Mary I
## 1516-1558

In her five-years as queen, 'Bloody' Mary went from hero to zero with the English public. She reversed the Protestant reforms her father and brother had made, bringing back the Catholic church. She had almost 300 Protestants burned at the stake, including the Archbishop of Canterbury, Thomas Cranmer. Brutal!

Mary made herself even more unpopular by marrying Prince Philip, King of Spain – people thought Spain would control England. But as Mary died without children, the throne eventually went to her half-sister, Elizabeth I.

## Bonus fact

Mary imprisoned future Queen Elizabeth I in the Tower of London for a time, just to show her who was boss.

# Elizabeth I
## 1533-1603

You've made it to the very last Tudor ruler!
Elizabeth I proved that women could
rule wisely and strongly (most men at the
time doubted it) – she struck terror into

her court with her sharp
wit and an even sharper
executioner's axe. She
turned around England's
finances by avoiding
wars when she could
and encouraging trade
to boost the country's
wealth (and pirates –
see page 112).

Elizabeth had many suitors, but turned them all down – she never married or had children.

**Bonus fact**

Elizabeth I paid attention to her public image. She boosted her 'brand' by going on at least 25 tours of her kingdom during her life, endearing herself to the English public.

**Now you've met all of the Tudor rulers, who would you choose to be your king or queen?**

# WOULD YOU RATHER

## act in a Tudor play

# OR take part in a jousting match?

WHAT WOULD YOU DO TO HAVE FUN IF YOU DIDN'T HAVE MOVIES, COMPUTER GAMES, TV, PHONES OR RADIO? IN TUDOR TIMES, ENTERTAINMENT CHOICES WERE LIMITED. FEW REGULAR TUDORS COULD READ, SO SEEING THINGS LIVE WAS THE ONLY OPTION. YOU HAD TO BE THERE ...

# Act in a Tudor play

Have you ever been in a play? If you made this choice, you'd be in for a very different experience than your regular modern-day theatre. Get ready!

Early Tudor plays were performed out in the street, until 1576, when actor John Burbage had the bright idea of building the first public theatre in London. He called it (drumroll please): The Theatre. Inventive . . .

Other theatres soon sprang up, each with their own company of actors. Tudor actors needed to be LOUD. Audiences would cheer, boo, whistle and heckle rudely. As an actor, you could feel free to shout equally rudely back over the racket! Actors would also need good reactions to duck out of the way of any rotten fruit or vegetables thrown at them from the rowdy crowd. Any female characters were played by men – no girl or women actors were allowed!

# Take part in
# a jousting match

Are you more of a sports fan than a theatre buff? Welcome to your first Tudor jousting match – I hope you've remembered your armour!

Jousting was the sport of kings and the king of sports in Tudor times. Tournaments thrilled the crowds who gathered to watch . . . but for the jousters themselves, it wasn't always so much fun.

Firstly, tournaments could be in far, far away places. If you weren't a local, you'd be riding your horse for days to get there, in all weathers.

When you arrived, saddle-sore and wet through, the last thing you probably wanted was to think horsey things – but your horse had to come first. Before you could think about resting yourself and getting a square meal, you'd need to finish grooming and feeding them.

Get ready for tournament day! You'd need to put on heavy armour weighing up to 45kg – that's like wearing a coat made of 108 full tins of baked beans!

After lots of processions and ceremony, you and your opponent would line up on either side of a cloth barrier, called the tilt, that ran the full length of the jousting field. You'd both be holding a long, hefty pole called a lance. With spectators watching from the sidelines, the pressure was on . . . at the signal, you would both CHARGE, galloping as fast as you could towards each other. The aim was to knock the pesky other knight

off his horse with one firm strike. *Boom*! The force of the lance that you and your speeding steed carried was huge. You'd better hope your armour could stand the impact. Some lances pierced the metal, and the soft squishy fleshy human inside. Henry VIII suffered two nasty accidents from jousting, once nearly losing his eye!

**To read about some more Tudor sports, turn the page . . .**

# TUDOR EXTRAS
## Sports report

Other than jousting, what sports could you play and watch in Tudor England? Be warned – like jousting, most of them were pretty violent!

### Cudgelling

Desperately simple and simply desperate. Two people would each be armed with a short club or stick, that they would use to try to hit their opponent's head. Points were scored each time a player drew blood!

## Archery

During the Tudor era, households had to keep bows and arrows in their home by law, including bows for children. Men were also ordered to practise their archery skills after going to church on a Sunday. You could even get pardoned if you accidentally shot someone while you were practising.

## 'Mob' football

Forget the Premier League – this game didn't feature VAR, penalties or 11 pampered players per side. The ball was a blown-up pig's stomach or bladder and the pitch was the open countryside space between two villages.

Each team could be made up of dozens, even hundreds of players.

The only rule was that . . . wait, there were no rules. The aim of the game wasn't to score goals but to get the ball into the centre of the other village. Biting, kicking, punching and strangling were all allowed. So was handball, as the ball could be picked up and run with, like in rugby. Watch out!

# WOULD YOU RATHER

## wipe Henry VIII's bottom

# OR be one of his wives?

KING HENRY VIII WAS A FIERY CHARACTER WITH A TERRIBLE TEMPER AND A PASSION FOR GETTING HIS OWN WAY. HOLDING A TRUSTED POSITION IN HIS COURT WAS A GOOD TACTIC TO STAY ON HIS GOOD SIDE. BUT IT DIDN'T GO TO PLAN FOR EVERYONE ...

# Wipe Henry's bottom

Congratulations! You've gained the king's trust and have been tasked with one of the most intimate jobs in the palace – the Groom of the Stool, who assisted the king on the toilet.* *Loo* had better look lively – the king is on his way for a toilet trip! Here's what to expect . . .

**STEP 1**

ENTER THE TOILET BEFORE HIS MAJESTY TO CHECK FOR ATTACKERS, THEN CLEAN ALL SURFACES, ESPECIALLY THE VELVET-PADDED TOILET SEAT.

*This sort of toilet would probably have been different to the one on page 17. It would likely have been a seat with a bowl or dish placed underneath to catch everything!

STEP 2

HELP HIS MAJESTY LOOSEN HIS CLOTHING AND SIT DOWN . . .

STEP 3

. . . PERHAPS OFFER THE KING ADVICE AND ENCOURAGEMENT AS HE HAD A POO.

STEP 4

WIPE THE ROYAL BOTTOM (IF HE COULDN'T BE BOTHERED).

**STEP 5**

FETCH WATER AND TOWELS FOR THE KING TO WASH HIS HANDS.

**STEP 6**

GIVE THE POO A THOROUGH INSPECTION AND TELL THE ROYAL PHYSICIAN (THE KING'S TOP DOCTOR) ALL ABOUT IT!

Far from being the worst job in the palace, top courtiers and nobles jostled for this position, hoping and praying that they or their son got the gig. Why? Because, getting that much access to the king in private was a dream job.

You would be totally trusted – meaning you could influence His Majesty's decisions about the kingdom, or receive titbits of top-secret information.

A Groom of the Stool wouldn't have to struggle in poverty – far from it. They could go on to bigger things. Henry VIII had four known Grooms of the Stool and each of them was knighted and given rewards or other top jobs.

When the Tudor boys finished ruling and Mary and Elizabeth took over, the job disappeared (though it would return with future kings later down the line). Instead, Ladies of the Bedchamber helped the queens take a bath (only once a month or so, mind) and brush their hair.

# Be one of Henry's wives

So you'd like to become a royal wife? Granted, it would probably be a less smelly choice. As far as we know, none of Henry VIII's six wives (yes, SIX) ever had to wipe his bottom. But, that doesn't mean being married to him was easy . . .

Henry began adulthood as a dashing, sporty young man. He spoke Spanish, French and Latin as well as English, composed songs and was a great dancer. But, he was also famed for his fearful temper, and it only got worse as he got older, heavier and grumpier. He could also be very cruel. Want proof? Let's meet the wives and find out . . .

## Catherine of Aragon: 1485-1536

DIVORCED

Catherine was originally married to Henry VIII's older brother, Arthur, but when he died, she became Henry's queen. In 1507, she became England's ambassador to Spain – the first known female ambassador in the whole of Europe. Catherine and Henry had six children, but only one of them survived to adulthood. Her name was Mary (see page 34 for more on her). Henry was desperate for a son to become his heir, and carry on the line of Tudor kings. Catherine didn't produce the son Henry wanted, so he ditched her. The brute! He also had his eye on someone else . . .

BEHEADED

### Anne Boleyn: 1501-1536

Anne was one of Catherine of Aragon's maids of honour when she caught Henry's eye. She spoke French, could dance well and played the lute. She was a bit of a Tudor rock star, but made many enemies at court. Plots against her mounted, and Henry gave her the chop. She was beheaded at the Tower of London by a skilled swordsman, leaving Henry with a daughter who later became Queen Elizabeth I (see page 36).

DIED

### Jane Seymour: 1509-1537

Eleven days after Anne Boleyn's execution, Henry married Jane. As a lady in waiting at the king's court, she may have had little choice in the matter. Henry was delighted when Jane gave birth to a son, Edward (see page 30). He had finally gained a male heir – but Jane sadly died two weeks later, after difficulties with the birth.

DIVORCED

## Anne of Cleves: 1515-1557

Henry chose Anne, daughter of the Duke of Cleves, as his next bride. They didn't even meet before they married – he only saw a painting of her. When she arrived in England, Henry realised she didn't look much like her profile picture – he didn't fancy her, nor she him. What's more, they didn't even speak the same language. Their marriage lasted six months before Anne waved *auf Wiedersehen*, keeping her head where it should be – on top of her neck.

BEHEADED

## Catherine Howard: 1524-1542

This Catherine was headstrong and outspoken, and she made enemies as soon as she married Henry in July 1540. She scrapped with Henry's daughter, Mary, and there were rumours she had been meeting her old boyfriend, Thomas Culpeper, in secret. This angered the king so it was off with Catherine's head, and Thomas's as well.

## Catherine Parr: 1512-1548

This Catherine was very patient, looking after the king who was very overweight and ill during their marriage. It appears Henry was truly grateful – she was given the queen's jewels and a whopping £7,000 a year for life after the king died in 1547. That's nearly £3 million in today's money – the average labourer earned just £2 per year. She also kept her head on her shoulders – result!

**So, there you have it. Would you want to marry your way to the top as the king's wife or work your way up from the, ahem, bottom as the Groom of the Stool? It's your call!**

# TUDORS EXTRAS
## Tudor tech

Europe in the 1500s and 1600s was a GREAT time for inventors. New, cool tech was popping up everywhere. Here are a few of the most exciting Tudor inventions . . .

### Flushing toilet

Sir John Harington was a poet, (though not a very good one), who got banned from the court of his godmother, Queen Elizabeth I, for telling rude stories. To get back into her good books, he put the rhymes aside and invented the first flushing water closet toilet. It worked! The queen was so *flushed* with

excitement at this new invention, she had one fitted in one of her favourite homes, Richmond Palace.

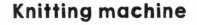

## Knitting machine

Tudor clothes were usually made of wool, but hand-knitted woolly clothing was slow to make. In 1589, William Lee invented a stocking frame: a machine that could knit with many needles at the same time, speeding up the process of making cloth.

## Invention imports

Lots of bright sparks across Europe were inventing great things in the Tudor age – from the first microscopes in the Netherlands to the first pocket watches in Germany. Printing, first invented in Germany, grew in popularity in England in the late 1400s. This resulted in the very first printed English books.

## Bonus fact

Robert Recorde was the royal physician (doctor) to both King Edward VI and Queen Mary I. In his spare time, he invented the equals sign. Recorde = legend!

# WOULD YOU RATHER

## go to Tudor school

# OR become an apprentice?

WHAT'S YOUR FAVOURITE LESSON AT SCHOOL? IN TUDOR TIMES, YOU MIGHT NOT HAVE HAD THE OPTION TO CHOOSE. SOME WEALTHY CHILDREN WENT TO SCHOOL, BUT MOST OF THEM STARTED WORKING FROM A YOUNG AGE AS APPRENTICES, PERHAPS TO A BAKER, CARPENTER OR GOLDSMITH. THEY'D HAVE COME OUT WITH SOME IMPRESSIVE SKILLS!

Is a Tudor classroom just right for you? If you think school in Tudor times was all work and no play . . . you'd be right.

School days began at 7am (ouch!) and could stretch on to 5 or 6pm. Oh, and there was school on Saturdays, too.

Schools mostly only accepted kids from well-off families. More boys than girls went to school – because Tudor women mostly spent their adult lives giving birth and caring for children, most parents didn't think it was worth them getting an education.*

The long lessons mostly involved memorising and repeating pieces of

*Some girls from rich families did their learning at home, where they were taught by private tutors

information over and over . . . again . . . and again . . . and . . .

**THWACK!** Any yawning or failure to perfectly repeat a long passage of a book back to the teacher, would see you get a whacking with a bundle of twigs.

Punishment aside, you would get to write with a cool feathery quill pen. Just make sure you don't smudge the ink, or you might get another round with the twigs . . .

# Become an apprentice

Welcome to your first day as an apprentice – better get your skates on, you've got a workshop to get to!

Tudor apprentices could work at any number of professions, from making clothing to shipbuilding. Shakespeare's dad was a glove-maker – bet he *gloved* his job! As a new apprentice, you'd start off doing all the horrible, mucky jobs at your new place of work as you learned your trade. You wouldn't even be paid for it – though you'd usually get a bed and meals provided by your employer.

Qualifying in your profession took a long time . . . you'd be working away for SEVEN YEARS before you finally earned the right to be paid as a regular worker. About time!

## Bonus fact

Being an apprentice was mostly for Tudor city kids – if you lived in the country, you'd likely start farming at seven or eight years of age, and keep going all the way through to adulthood!

**These weren't all the Tudor jobs you could do - head to page 104 to find out about some seriously sneaky jobs . . .**

# TUDORS EXTRAS
## William Shakespeare

The most famous English playwright ever was a Tudor. William Shakespeare was born in Stratford-upon-Avon in 1564, and had his first work – a long poem – published in 1593. It wasn't his last, Will just couldn't stop writing. In all, he wrote around 38 plays that we know about, and 154 sonnets (a type of poem).

Will joined the Lord Chamberlain's Men – a company of actors who, in 1599, opened the Globe Theatre in London. But, catastrophe struck in 1613 when the theatre burned down whilst one of Will's plays was being performed. A cannon used in the play set the theatre's thatched roof ablaze! Thankfully, the theatre was rebuilt within a year – this time with a tiled roof. Good choice.

Will's way with words was awesome and still influences writers today. In fact, you almost definitely use some of the hundreds of new words and phrases he made popular. Want to find out more? Turn the page . . .

This is a GREAT idea!

# Spot the Shakespeare

Shakespeare's impact on the English language is enormous. He invented or popularised many words and phrases that we use today. On the page opposite are six words and phrases that Shakespeare invented (some of them he made into a new form, like an adjective). There are also four that he didn't. Can you spot the Shakespearean words? To check your answers, look at the bottom of the opposite page.

For a bonus point, try writing your own story, play or poem using some (or all) of these words!

GLOOMY

BITE THE BULLET

SUITCASE

WILD GOOSE CHASE

MAIDEN

DENIM

SWAGGER

BLUSHING

LUGGAGE

MOUNTAINEER

# WOULD YOU RATHER

eat frog
blancmange
for dinner

# OR the mysterious cockentrice?

WHAT PEOPLE ATE IN TUDOR TIMES DEPENDED VERY MUCH ON HOW RICH THEY WERE. IF YOU WERE POOR, THE BEST YOU COULD HOPE FOR WOULD PROBABLY BE A BARELY-COOKED TURNIP OR SOME WATERY STEW. BUT, RICH TUDORS ATE ALL SORTS OF EXOTIC DISHES! GET READY FOR AN UNFORGETTABLE BANQUET...

# Eat frog blancmange

Do you like your dinner extra froggy?
Better *hop* to it!

Rich Tudors held feasts with all kinds
of unusual and extravagant dishes.
Forget beans on toast – on a Tudor
menu, you could find roasted swan and
peacock, baked conger eel and boiled
porpoise*. The main porpoise – *ahem*,
purpose – was not only to feed guests but
to show off their mighty wealth.

They also liked to mix up sweet
and savoury things in the same dish.
Blancmange is eaten today as a type of

*Henry VIII's first wife, Catherine of Aragon, enjoyed a bit of
porpoise for her dinner.

wobbly dessert, but in the time of the Tudors, it was a main course. Instead of sweet flavourings, it would be filled with chunks of chicken meat.

On some days of the year, meat wasn't allowed to be eaten for religious reasons, so the Tudors replaced the chicken in the blancmange with whole frogs! And no, not just in *leap* years . . .

# Eat a cockentrice

Did you choose this unlikely looking beast? Are you just wondering what it really is? Let's take a closer look . . .

The cockentrice was a seriously bizarre bit of cooking, designed to look like a mythological beast from the myths and legends of medieval Europe. It's believed that it was first served by Henry VIII's kitchens to impress King Francis I of France, when the two kings met in 1520. The feast's shopping list included more than 2,000 sheep, 98,000 eggs and three porpoises. That's a lot of grub!

To make a cockentrice, Henry's cooks took a suckling pig, sawed it in half and sewed it onto the body of a large capon (a sort of fattened-up chicken).

Later in the Tudor era, cockentrices were half-pig, half-turkey. You could call it a *pork-ey*! Turkeys made a bigger and more impressive-looking cockentrice, but they only arrived when Spanish sailors brought them back to Europe from North America.

**If you've still got a bit of room left after all that food, turn the page for dessert!**

# TUDOR EXTRAS
## A sugary treat

Do you like a pudding or a sweet treat? Wealthy Tudors definitely did – they couldn't get enough of it! Sugar became all the rage in the 1500s, with traders importing tonnes of it from South America and the Caribbean to satisfy booming demand. Only for the rich, though, mind you – poor people had to make do with honey as a sweetener. One Tudor earl ordered 900kg of sugar in a single year just for himself!

Henry VIII employed a confectioner, whose job was to handle sugar and turn it into elaborate sweet treats for His Majesty. What a sweet job!

Cardinal Wolsey (see page 118) went one step further and entertained French visitors with over 100 giant sculptures all made of sugar paste. Sugar castles, sugar birds, and even a sugar cathedral. They looked good enough to eat . . . and were!

The trouble with this sudden sugar rush can be summed up in one equation:

Sugar + more sugar − toothbrushes − toothpaste = BIG problems.

Tudor teeth turned black with decay and, for a while, black gnashers were fashionable, as they showed you ate a lot of sugar, so must be fabulously wealthy.

The one positive side to a Tudor toothache was that it definitely wouldn't lead to a visit to the dentists. Why? Because there weren't any.

It might, though, mean a quick trip to a quack – a person who pretended to be a doctor and sold 'cures'. These would be a mixture of herbs, pepper and other natural ingredients. Not so bad to eat, but they very rarely worked.

You might make your own remedies at home, such as tooth soap, a powder that you'd gently rub onto your teeth. The only trouble was making it in the first place – tooth soap's only ingredient was dead mouse heads which were burned then crushed into a powder. *Yuck!*

The last (and worst) option was to visit a barber-surgeon. How would you find them? By the screams coming from their shop! They'd use metal pliers to yank out any rotten teeth. With no painkillers – *owwww!*

# WOULD YOU RATHER

**cure yourself by strapping a chicken to your head**

# OR by letting leeches suck your blood?

NO, THESE WEREN'T PRANKS ON A TUDOR REALITY SHOW. THESE WERE MEDICAL TREATMENTS SUGGESTED BY SERIOUS DOCTORS! IN TUDOR TIMES, DISEASE WAS HARD TO AVOID, PARTLY BECAUSE OF CROWDED, UNCLEAN CONDITIONS IN CITIES, PARTLY BECAUSE PEOPLE DIDN'T KNOW THAT MUCH ABOUT DISEASES. IF YOU WERE UNLUCKY ENOUGH TO GET ILL, YOU COULD EXPECT SOME NASTY TREATMENTS ...

# Cure yourself with a chicken

Waves of deadly plague had swept through England before the Tudors, and they were still terrified of it. With good reason – an outbreak of plague in 1563 killed more than a quarter of all those who lived in the City of London.

The Tudors didn't realise that plague was spread by bacteria carried by fleas and rats. Because they didn't really understand where it came from, many of their cures weren't very helpful.

One of the oddest remedies was suggested by King Henry VIII's surgeon, Thomas Vicary. It started with plucking the feathers from the bottom of a live chicken! Then, the bare-bottomed bird would be strapped to your head (or any other infected body part). It's possible that Tudor medics thought that chickens breathe through their bottoms, and would suck the plague out of infected body parts!

Another cure for plague was collecting you and your family's farts in an airtight jar. The idea was that if you got the plague, you'd open the jar and take in long breaths of the stinky air to cleanse yourself. *Urgh*!

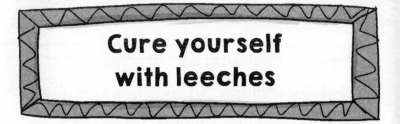

# Cure yourself
# with leeches

Blood-letting (literally, letting blood flow out of the body) was the closest thing the Tudors had to a cure-all, and doctors used it to treat all kinds of diseases.

There were several ways blood-letting could occur. The first involved using a super sharp blade to make cuts into parts of your body to let the blood flow out. Doctors decided which body part to cut by checking your birthday or how the stars in the sky were lined up. No, seriously!

Instead of being all cut up, you might be covered in lethal leeches, who would suck the blood out. These little worms have suckers with sharp teeth that can chomp

through flesh, making
a Y-shaped bite.

A leech can gulp down
around 3-10 times its own
bodyweight in blood. After its
feast, it would be stored in a jar – it
wouldn't want another meal for
months! If you got haemorrhoids
(a painful swelling of blood
vessels around and inside the
hole in your bottom)
you'd be prescribed
as many as 20 leeches
on your bum a week.
Doubt you'd want to sit
down after that!

**Go back to page 20 for
a reminder of some more
Tudor cures!**

# TUDOR EXTRAS
## Tudor toilets

Tudor loos were not high tech. They were often holes in the ground called cesspits and privies (see page 16) – but some people didn't even have these!

Many people in busy Tudor towns didn't have land to dig holes for cesspits, so they used an indoor privy. This was a seat with a hole in it and a chamber pot below to catch all the wee and poo. Others just had the pot and kept it stored under the bed.

The pot had to be emptied, of course. Most Tudors did that in one simple action . . . chucking the pot's contents out of the window into the street.

Watch out below!
The phrase, 'gardy
loo!' was often
shouted as a warning
before the waste
rained down. It stems
from the French,
*prenez garde a l'eau!*
meaning 'beware of
the water'. Only, it
wasn't just water that
might hit you . . .
*Yuck*!

Gardy loo!

# WOULD YOU RATHER

## be caught gossiping

# OR not wearing a hat on a Sunday?

THERE WERE NO POLICE OFFICERS IN TUDOR TIMES, BUT CRIMINALS WEREN'T OFF THE HOOK. WOE BETIDE YOU IF YOU WERE CAUGHT! PUNISHMENTS WERE OFTEN MUCH HARSHER THAN A SIMPLE FINE OR TELLING-OFF. FOR EXAMPLE, IF YOU STOLE SOMETHING WORTH LESS THAN A SHILLING (ABOUT 5P TODAY), YOU COULD BE WHIPPED PAINFULLY IN FRONT OF YOUR NEIGHBOURS. OUCH!

# Be caught gossiping

Did you choose to go for a good gossip?
Ouch! The Tudors had a low opinion of
people spreading rumours about others.
Even claiming someone had sold you
a bad fish or rotten fruit was considered
a crime.

If they were found guilty, the accused
could be forced to wear a 'brank' (also
known as a scold's bridle). This was
a heavy iron frame that was locked
around your head for up to a day. It had
a metal bit (a kind of prong) that went
into your mouth and pressed down
on your tongue, stopping you from
speaking. Some bits had a metal spike

which cut into your tongue if you tried to speak. *Ow!* Some bridles also had a bell to alert others you were nearby.

The Tudors liked their punishments to be in public so everyone could see what would happen if they did the same thing. They thought it acted as a warning.

My apples are fine, thank you very much!

Did this Tudor crime really catch your *hat*-tention? In 1571, it became the law for every boy and man to wear a cap or hat made of wool on Sundays and holidays. (Top nobles were exempt.)

Those caught hatless could be fined many days' wages. If they didn't have the money, they'd be placed in stocks or pillories for hours at a time, with their

legs or head and arms locked in place. In stocks, you sat down while you were locked in. Pillories were more painful – you'd have to stand, so would have a bent back and sore neck all day. Stocks and pillories were usually placed in the centre of villages or towns so everyone could see you – and throw things at you!

**Better try to avoid punishments altogether! Some sentences were even worse though . . . turn the page to find out.**

# TUDOR EXTRAS
## Which witch is which?

You *really* wouldn't want to be labelled a witch in the Tudor era. These were superstitious times and people were terrified of anything they didn't understand. Witches were blamed for anything bad that happened – from milk going sour to the plague.

Being a witch was a crime, punishable by DEATH! But how did the Tudors work out who was a witch? Here are a few questions that Tudors asked to point them in the right direction . . .

# Witchfinders Manual
## Finding a Witch

- Is your suspect a woman?

- Is she old or ugly?

- Does she have strange marks on her face?*

- Does she talk to herself?

- Does she live alone?

- Does an animal, like a black cat, follow her around?

- Is she ever seen without a shadow?

None of these things should be a crime, or even thought of as unusual. Women often outlasted men in age, so of course they lived on their own and sometimes had pet cats and talked to themselves.

* These could be anything from birthmarks to smallpox scars.

But that didn't stop distrustful villagers from accusing lone women of being witches. And once that happened, things turned very nasty indeed . . .

One witch test, involving a dunk in the local river, was a real lose-lose option. A suspect was 'ducked' into deep

water. If she couldn't swim and sank,
she was thought to be innocent . . .
but she'd also be dead from drowning.
If she bobbed back up to the surface,
some supernatural power was thought
to have kept her afloat, meaning . . .
WITCH! Hardly fair.

# WOULD YOU RATHER

be Queen Elizabeth I's master of spies

# OR one of her official pirates?

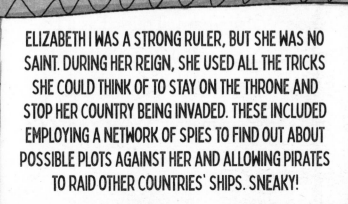

ELIZABETH I WAS A STRONG RULER, BUT SHE WAS NO SAINT. DURING HER REIGN, SHE USED ALL THE TRICKS SHE COULD THINK OF TO STAY ON THE THRONE AND STOP HER COUNTRY BEING INVADED. THESE INCLUDED EMPLOYING A NETWORK OF SPIES TO FIND OUT ABOUT POSSIBLE PLOTS AGAINST HER AND ALLOWING PIRATES TO RAID OTHER COUNTRIES' SHIPS. SNEAKY!

# Master of spies

Do you spy with your little eye . . . a real-life Tudor spy!?

Elizabeth I was a popular queen with many people, but she also experienced a lot of plotting against her, often by those who didn't like her Protestant religion. If these plots had been successful, they would have seen her lose her throne . . . and maybe even her head. Some of these plots were foiled by a cunning Tudor gentleman named Sir Francis Walsingham. Trained as a lawyer, Sir Francis was a diplomat and royal advisor – but, in secret, he was also the world's first spymaster. What a job title!

He built up a network of more than 50 spies and informers around England and mainland Europe. These useful contacts told him of any plots and plans being hatched and any alliances being formed by enemies of England.

Sir Francis pioneered some of the spy skills used today in the modern world. He set up a code-breaking department to uncover the meaning of secret messages and used double agents who pretended to spy for the enemy but instead were spying for him!

In 1586, Mary, Queen of Scots and Sir Anthony Babington made top secret plans to overthrow Elizabeth I – the Babington Plot. Their secret messages were hidden in a beer barrel and carried by a messenger. But, the messenger was actually one of Sir Francis' double agents. Sneaky! The plot was foiled and both Mary and Babington were executed.

As a successful spymaster, you would be trusted greatly and rewarded well.

But you would always have to stay vigilant for the next threat . . . and the next one after that. It would have been exhausting, time-consuming work. You'd have to keep your job secret, too – so no bragging about it!

Now you've found out about Francis,
how about doing some code-cracking
yourself? Below is a message encoded
using a substitution cipher. Each letter
has been swapped for a number, so A=1,
B=2, C=3 and so on, until Z=26.
Can you reveal the hidden message?
To check the answer, look at
the bottom of the
next page.

6 18 1 14 3 9 19
23
8 1 19
19 20 9 14 11 25,
3 8 5 5 19 25
6 5 5 20!

SOLUTION: FRANCIS W HAS STINKY, CHEESY FEET!

# Official pirate

*Arrrrrr* you a sailor extraordinaire? Grab your sword, buckle your boots and let's head out to sea!

Elizabeth I's pirates weren't actually called pirates – their official job title was 'privateer' (it sounded a bit more noble). But, there was nothing honest or noble about what they did – mostly storming onto other people's ships and stealing all their loot.

Privateers would sail the same routes as European trading ships that were loaded up with treasures from places like western Africa, the Caribbean and South America.

Once they'd spotted a ship, they'd sail up close to their prey, let rip with their ship's cannons and pound the unsuspecting vessel with fire. Helpfully, most trading ships didn't put up much of a fight. So, soon the fierce privateers would be aboard, stealing the treasure.

Privateers usually had other jobs, such as trading, and did a bit of piracy in their spare time. Turn the page to read about three of the most famous ones . . .

## Sir Martin Frobisher

Fearless Martin Frobisher harassed French trading ships off the coast of Guinea, in western Africa. He later sailed far north to chilly Canada, where he found deposits of rocky ore he thought contained gold. Result! He returned to England with more than 1,000 tonnes of the stuff, but after years of processing the ore, it was discovered to be worthless. *Doh*!

## Henry Strangewishe

Also known as Henry Strangways, Henry's favourite activity was plundering Spanish treasure ships just before they got home. He was imprisoned multiple times in England but Elizabeth always

pardoned him. He had friends in
high places!

### Sir Francis Drake

Sir Francis was a key figure in Elizabeth
I's court, and mixed his explorations
with a fair bit of plundering. In 1572,
Francis and his crew attacked Spanish
ships loaded with precious metals. They
sailed away with silver worth about
£30 million at today's prices. Queen
Elizabeth was very pleased!

**Would you enjoy a life at sea?
To find out about someone who
made their living beneath the
waves, turn to page 122.**

# Top Tudors hall of fame

Welcome to the Tudor hall of fame –
this time for non-royals! The kings and
queens might have been the most well-
known and famous Tudors in the land,
but there were some other celebs who
weren't far behind them. There were
scientists, religious officials, politicians,
rebels and many more – and some made
a real impact on the country. Once
you've got to the end, you can decide –
which one of these famous four would
you rather get an autograph from?

# Cardinal Thomas Wolsey
## 1475-1530

This butcher's son rose to become the second most important person in England, behind Henry VIII. The young king was often more interested in hunting, sports and feasting than ruling England, leaving Thomas to get on with running things . . . exactly how *he* wanted.

Wolsey grew fabulously rich and lived like a king, building a 280-room palace called Hampton Court that you can still visit today. (Not its a-*maze*-ing maze, though, that came 180 years later.)

In 1528, Wolsey gave the palace to Henry VIII, to try and keep himself in the king's good books. Unfortunately, it didn't work – two years later, Henry had him executed!

# Anne Askew

Anne was a true Tudor rebel. She was deeply religious and read the Bible – an action Henry VIII had declared illegal for women. Meanie! Anne was also one of the first female English poets and writers we know about.

Her religion led her to become one of the first Tudor women to demand a divorce – she became a Protestant and wanted to leave her Catholic husband. Anne travelled to London where Henry VIII refused her request for a divorce and sent spies to keep a watch on her. Eek! An independent woman with her own views on religion was considered dangerous. In 1546, poor Anne became the only woman to be tortured in the Tower of London and then burned at the stake.

# Jacques Francis

This top Tudor may not have been that well known during his lifetime, but he helped to rescue some prize military possessions . . .

Henry VIII's favourite warship, the *Mary Rose*, saw her last battle in 1545 – she was attacked by French ships and sank down, down, down to the bottom of the sea. Henry VIII was NOT pleased – around £2 million worth of guns (in today's money) had sunk with it. But, all was not lost! Salvage divers were commissioned to rescue as much of the sunken equipment as they could. In one of these teams was expert swimmer, Jacques Francis, from Guinea in West Africa. Considering most Tudors couldn't swim at all, he had great skill! He likely dived without any equipment – just taking a deep, deep breath before he plunged down. Jacques is also known for being the first Black person we know of to give evidence in an English law court – he testified in support of one of his colleagues who had been accused of stealing.

# John Dee

Science was very mixed up with myth and superstition in Tudor England. Dee was an astronomer and mathematician, but he also told fortunes and produced horoscopes for clients including Queen Mary I. Queen Elizabeth I made him her Royal Advisor in Mystic Secrets – what a great job title! Dee advised Elizabeth on everything from what day she should be crowned (he chose the 15th January, 1559) to where she should send ships to explore.

He built up the biggest personal library in England during his life – but books weren't his only passion. He spent some of his time performing alchemy, the art of trying to turn metals like lead and copper into gold . . . unsuccessfully!

**Which top Tudor is getting your autograph request?**

# WOULD YOU RATHER

## fill your pants with stuffing

# OR get poked by your many bumroll pins?

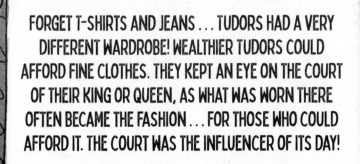

FORGET T-SHIRTS AND JEANS ... TUDORS HAD A VERY DIFFERENT WARDROBE! WEALTHIER TUDORS COULD AFFORD FINE CLOTHES. THEY KEPT AN EYE ON THE COURT OF THEIR KING OR QUEEN, AS WHAT WAS WORN THERE OFTEN BECAME THE FASHION ... FOR THOSE WHO COULD AFFORD IT. THE COURT WAS THE INFLUENCER OF ITS DAY!

# Fill your pants with stuffing

Do you think some really big pants would suit you perfectly? You'd be extremely fashionable amongst wealthy Tudor men!

In Tudor court, it became fashionable to look as grand and as BIG as possible. The logic was that if you looked huge, people would assume you were also extremely powerful!

Adult men went out in short pants called hose, which they plumped up with stuffing until they were the size and shape of pumpkins. This stuffing was called bombast and could be made of scraps of cloth, horsehair (itchy!) or tiny linen fibres called bran. This could absorb a lot of water, meaning a rainy day could leave you with soggy bulges sloshing around your legs.

Even *more* padding was used in the front of men's doublets (box-shaped jackets) which were worn over a shirt. And as if that wasn't enough, a cloak made up of many metres of cloth would be plonked on top. You'd look enormous – which was the general idea!

# Get poked by bumroll pins

Are you feeling *pin*-spired by the clothes of Tudor noblewomen? Hope you are patient – getting dressed could take a while . . .

But what's a bumroll, you ask? *Bumroll*, please . . . it was a padded roll of material worn around your hips and under your dress to hold the skirt in place. This was just one of a LOT of different garments that wealthy Tudor women wore every day. Luckily for them, they had servants to help them dress!

# Dressing to-do list:

PUT ON STOCKINGS, EARRINGS AND SHOES.

SLIDE CHEMISE* OVER THE TOP.

ADD A PETTICOAT FOR EXTRA WARMTH.

*This was a neck-to-floor shirt, often made of linen, or if you were royal, silk. It was the main item of underwear – Tudor women didn't wear knickers.

CLIMB INTO A FARTHINGALE: A BARREL-SHAPED FRAME DESIGNED TO HOLD OUT THE BOTTOM PART OF THE SKIRT.

SQUEEZE INTO A CORSET STIFFENED WITH WOODEN SLATS.

← Not very comfy!

PUT A PARTLET ON TOP OF THE CORSET, TO COVER THE SHOULDERS.

I'm tired already.

TIE A BUMROLL AROUND THE HIPS TO MAKE THE SKIRT AND GOWN FLARE OUT.

PUT ON A KIRTLE (THE MAIN UNDERSKIRT).

DRAPE A GOWN OVER THE LOT

Nearly there...

PIN OR SEW ON SLEEVES.

Ouch!

PIN ON NECK RUFF.

ADD A HEADDRESS OR HAT.

Oops, nearly forgot.

PUT LITTLE TINY RUFFS ON WRISTS.

Curses. I took so long, I missed the ball.

That's a lot of clothes. Each item was handmade, expensive and often needed a LOT of pins to hold it in place.

The farthingale was a cage made of wooden or whalebone hoops. It helped transform ladies' skirts and dresses into large, eye-catching bell shapes. Cage is a good word – when the fashion changed to favour bigger and broader farthingales (up to 1.2m wide), some ladies felt a bit trapped inside their clothing.

The bulkiness and heaviness of fine clothing made movement difficult. Sitting down and getting through small doorways was tricky too, especially with all those pins in the bumroll and other clothing layers, ready and waiting to stick into your bottom. *Oww!*

So, are you prepared to be *sharply* dressed with lots of pointy pins? Or are some big pants the *stuff* for you?

# TUDORS EXTRAS
## Ruff stuff

During Elizabeth I's reign, ruffs became all the rage for men and women. They were made of dozens of folds of lace (or linen, if you weren't quite so wealthy). It was kept stiff with a sticky substance called starch – and, of course, it was kept in place using dozens of pins to hold all the frills.

In the 1580s and 1590s, ruffs grew and grew in size until they got really quite silly. Some ruffs were more than 20cm deep. Wearers couldn't see their own feet! Special spoons with extra-long handles had to be developed so people could eat while wearing their ruffs.

If you got caught in the rain, you could end up in a *ruff* situation. All that starch powder would run straight down like runny pastry over all your other fine clothes. What's worse, your ruff would go limp and people might laugh at you. Oh, the shame!

# How it all ended

On 24th March 1603, Elizabeth I died, aged 69. She'd done well to hang on as long as she had. Most Tudors only lived about half as long!

Elizabeth never married or had children. She had also outlived all of her father Henry VIII's other children. So, who would succeed her as ruler? This caused a lot of hushed debate as various nobles jostled to be next on the throne.

In the end, Elizabeth's cousin, King James VI of Scotland, got the nod. He hopped on a horse, galloped south and became King James I of England in 1603. From here on, England was no longer run by the House of Tudor – it was now controlled by the House of Stuart, an era that lasted for over one hundred years.

It nearly came to a swift end, though. Like Elizabeth, James was a Protestant and continued to stop Catholics from worshipping. Just two years into his reign, an infamous plot was hatched by a group of Catholics to blow the king up whilst he was visiting the Houses of Parliament. Fortunately, the plot was foiled. One of the conspirators, Guy Fawkes, was caught red-handed in a cellar below the House of Lords along with firewood, fuses and some 36 barrels of gunpowder. Game's up, Guy. That would have been an explosive ending!

# Glossary

**Alliance** – an agreement between people or countries to work or fight together.

**Ambassador** – a person who represents their country abroad.

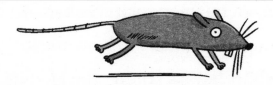

**Bombast** – material used for padding Tudor clothes.

**Catholic** – short for Roman Catholic – someone who follows a branch of the Christian religion headed by the Pope.

**Court** – the place where a king or queen lives, and a name given to all the servants and advisors who serve them.

**Latin** – an ancient language used by the Romans. In Tudor times, it was the most commonly used language for writing, law and religion.

**Monastery** – a building (or group of buildings) in which monks live, work and worship.

**Nobles** – rich and important people who owned a lot of land. They often had titles like Earl or Duke.

**Peasants** – people who worked on the land. Some owned a small strip of land but most worked for landowners. Nearly all peasants were poor.

**Plague** – an infectious disease carried by fleas that live on rats. The disease was deadly in Tudor times.

**Privateer** – a sailor who had permission from his country's ruler to attack other countries' ships and steal their cargoes.

**Protestant** – a follower of a branch of the Christian religion separate from Roman Catholicism.

**Rebellion** – when a group of people rise up against the people running the country and try to replace them.

# About the author

Clive Gifford grew up in the shadow of Windsor Castle and learnt lots about the Tudors at school, as a teenaged tour guide taking visitors around Hampton Court and as an adult, writing exciting history books for adults and children. Clive has scribbled and typed more than 200 books and has won the Royal Society, SLA and Blue Peter book awards. Unlike Henry VIII, Clive is perfectly happy having just the one wife, Jane, and lives in Manchester, UK.

# About the illustrator

As a young boy, Tim Wesson was constantly doodling, finding any excuse to put pen to paper. Since turning his much-loved pastime into his profession, Tim has achieved great success in the world of children's publishing, having illustrated and authored books across a variety of formats. He takes great delight in turning the world on its head and inviting children to go on the adventure with him.

**Explore the rest of the series for more fascinating facts and hilarious WOULD YOU RATHER questions!**

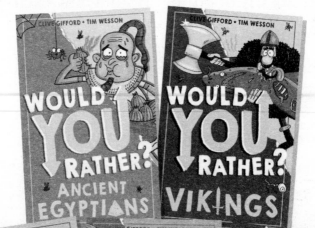